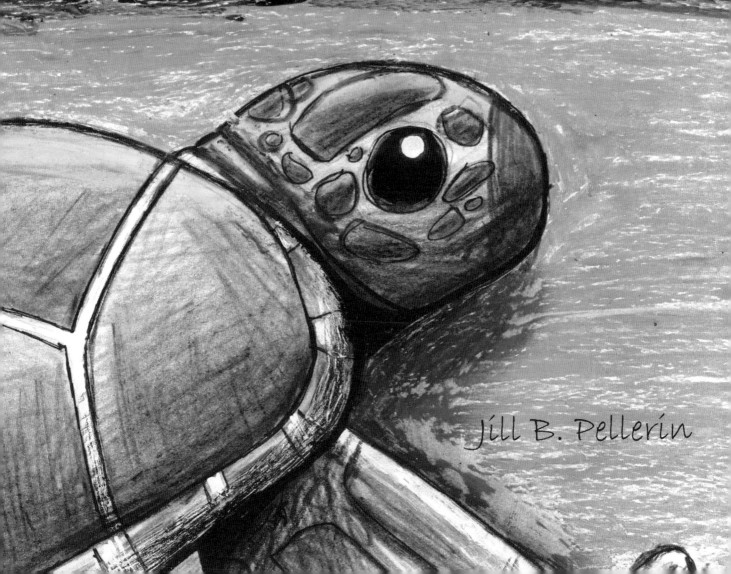

Brighter Horizon

A SEA TURTLE'S JOURNEY

Jill B. Pellerin

Some of the proceeds of the sale of this product will go to benefit the Pokot orphans of Kenya, Africa.

With deep appreciation
To

Mark S. Pritchett
For his continuous support

Wilma Katz
For introducing me to the sea turtles' world

&

Lindsay Pellerin
For tireless work on the illustrations

Our world is full of amazing animals. It is a beautiful thing to live side by side with them.

Let us remember that everyday we need to respect and take responsibility for the planet we live on.

The lily is a symbol of purity and beauty. Each picture has a lily hidden somewhere. See if you can find it and remember God's creations are everywhere.

Introduction

Sea turtle hatchlings have a multitude of obstacles when they emerge. All of them are life threatening.

There are natural enemies but man has caused threats to the turtles' world.

For many years the author of this book has lived in coastal areas with an awareness of the endangered sea turtles. The summer of 2009 allowed Jill to participate in the monitoring and the awareness of these turtles while living on Florida's west coast. One day on a "nest excavation" a tiny green sea turtle was gently lifted from its sand nest with a crippled front flipper. Her daughter asked, "Will she make it?" Jill knew the chances were slimmer than 1000 to 1 but a story came to her head that said, "Yes....yes, this turtle *will* make it!" So began the story of Enola and her unlikely survival journey.

This is the tale of a very determined turtle and, like any child with a physical hurdle to overcome; there will be a lot of adapting to do.

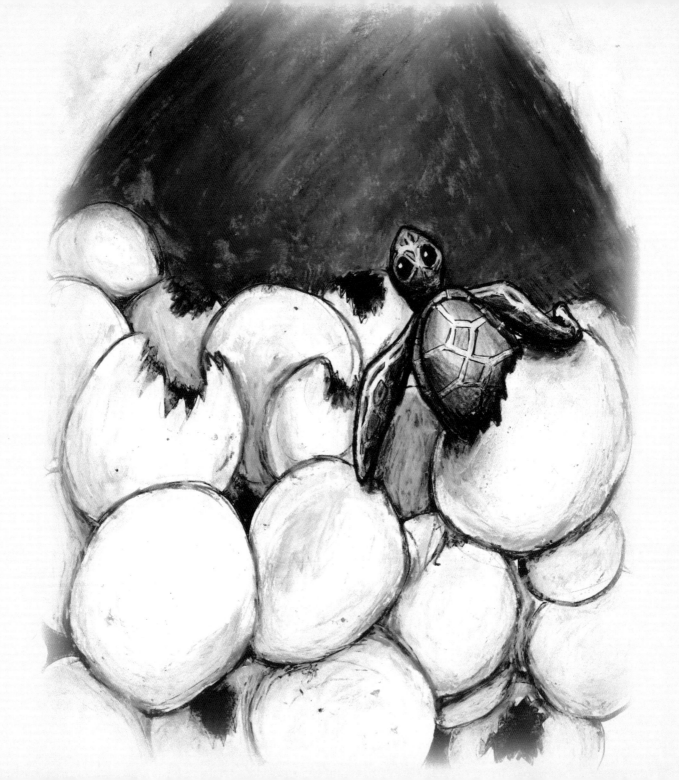

Activity was high about two feet down into the warm sand on a quiet Florida beach. It had been about 50 days since a beautiful green sea turtle laid 115 pearly white eggs in a hole she dug herself. She returned to the gulf waters never to see her hatchlings born. Enola could sense the hasty movement of all her brothers and sisters around her. This was an urgent mass escape out of the sand nest. At night the cooler sands stirred the turtles. Their need to head for the water was strong.

Enola was aware she could not scramble as quickly as she wanted, while others scurried upward leaving her behind. After a few hours the nest was silent. As the sun came up it warmed the sand and Enola went into a much needed sleep.

Suddenly there was sunlight and a sensation of being scooped up from the sand nest. A large, gloved hand examined the wiggling turtle. The concerned turtle volunteer noticed a bent front flipper as he put Enola in a bucket of damp sand.

Nearby was a young, red-haired boy. He was born without fingers on his right hand but his curiosity about life never stopped him from exploring. He peered into the bucket. "This tiny turtle has a flipper that is different. We are alike! Will she make it?" The kind man just smiled at the boy. He knew he must set the turtle free that night and with an already slim chance to survive, this one surely would not make it.

Shuffle – flap, shuffle – flap ….. Making her way in the dark of night, Enola made her imprint on the cool wet sand of the beach. This would be a key to returning to this very spot when she was older.

The little green sea turtle limped toward a bright horizon way off in the distance. There was a strong instinct pulling her out to a deep, dark, sea.

Paddling a bit unsteadily with her bent flipper, Enola swam out for many hours until she came to a weed line. These weeds were called sargassum. This would be her floating home for the next ten years.

Here she would find warmth, food and safety. It was important to play and grow here. She would soon learn that she was in a world full of creatures that might harm her. In the weed line Enola would spend the "lost years" drifting thousands of miles where ever the ocean's currents might take her. She would grow bigger and stronger before new adventures took her elsewhere.

Time came for Enola to break away from her weed home. She had grown bigger and now she would be safer in the open waters. Instincts were calling her for adventures. Even the bent flipper could not hold her back. These waters were still very dark and deep so she headed where she knew there would be comfort.

One day while exploring Enola became aware of a large, lurking shadow. Sensing danger she swam as fast as she could. A huge shark with very sharp teeth was chasing the little turtle. Her one bent flipper caused her to swim in a crazy path which confused the shark and she ducked for safety in a rock cave.

Making her way to calmer water, the little green turtle spotted a school of fish. How much fun it would be to swim and dart about. Enola gave it a try. Turtles can swim fast for a short time but soon the yellow fish swam far ahead.

Then, without warning, a loud *swoosh* and a cloud of bubbles stopped Enola's chase. An octopus had grabbed one of the pretty fish. This was scary for the small turtle as she made a quick turn upward toward the surface to get some air.

Enola's flipper had saved her once again as she couldn't swim as fast as the sleek fish.

Enola swam onward. The sea became shallow and warmer. There were lots of grasses to feed upon among the pretty coral.

One day while hiding and munching in the sea grass, the green turtle stuck her head out and was looking right in the face of a beautiful fish. It was a friendly face. They became playmates for the day, eating and swimming about the lovely coral. This made the turtle realize she had been living her years alone.

Did you ever think about Enola spelled backward? It spells *alone*. Turtles do spend their days surrounded by other sea creatures, but they basically live their lives by themselves and not in turtle groups.

Enola is a Native American Indian name. It means alone.

All sea turtles do certain things to take care of themselves. Eating is a big part of a turtle's life. Enola could eventually weigh 300 pounds! Her diet is mainly the plants she finds in the ocean.

One day while chewing on sea grass, along the corals, Enola bit into something very different. She could not tear it. It was very rubbery. She bit and pulled and pulled. She paddled backward but her bent flipper did not give her the strength she needed. Soon she gave up and swam away for something easier to chew. This was a good thing because the grass was actually a balloon and it would harm Enola if she would have swallowed it.

The sunshine is another attraction for the adult sea turtles. Enola loved to crawl up on the warm sand from time to time, even though she normally basked while floating in the water. Basking is what turtles do to soak up some sun. Laying very still in the sunlight allows the sea turtles to store much needed heat.

It is important for these reptiles to have warmth and air. This made Enola feel rested and ready for more swimming in the cold waters.

In order for sea turtles to keep themselves clean they rely on some of their fellow sea creatures to help.

Enola was feeling like she was getting heavy. It was getting harder to escape her enemies. She called upon some fish friends to clean her so she would have less drag. The fish gathered atop her shell and ate all the tiny seaweed growing on the turtle's back.

After Enola's shell was cleaned she could once again zip through the water, as fast as her one good flipper would allow.

Enola had many years of swimming and playing and growing to be an adult.

She had been able to beat the odds so far and her bent flipper had helped her escape a lot of dangers. Enola was big enough now that she had very few enemies but one day she swam right under one of the biggest dangers of all sea turtles….fishermen's nets!

She looked up with awe and fright of all the things trapped forever in this tangle of net. This big bundle had fish, bottles, seaweeds, sea jellies and the saddest sight was a loggerhead turtle trapped inside. This net was freely floating through the ocean and was called a "ghost net".

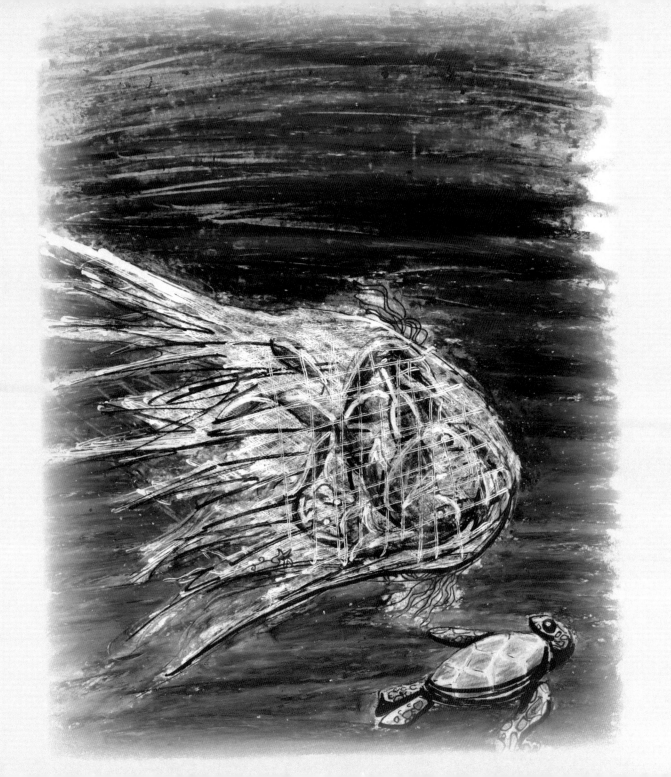

Enola was an adult now and felt a calling to return to the place where her life began so many years ago.

She really didn't understand this urge but had one more discovery before she could return to that beautiful Florida beach.

This discovery was a big, handsome male turtle who decided he liked Enola. They swam around together for most of the day, flirting in their turtle ways. Their mating would help Enola's turtle eggs grow lots of tiny hatchlings.

The attraction was over and the mission to swim hard and fast to the beach was strong. The green sea turtle was heading to the beach where she was born.

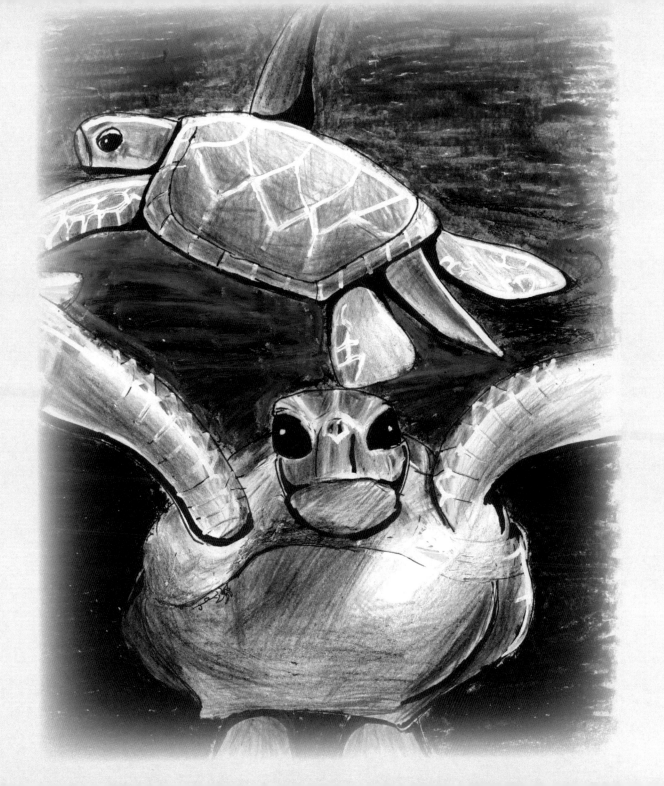

Sitting in the sand dunes late one night a grown man looked down at his hand which never had fingers. His life had been very successful for he overcame this challenge of an imperfect hand. He thought back to 25 years ago when he saw a tiny turtle with a bent flipper and felt they were alike.

"I wonder what ever became of that turtle," was his thought. He glanced out to the water's edge and noticed a large-shelled creature crawling ashore. It was Enola making her way up the beach to lay her clutch of eggs and fulfill her life's duty.

In the dark night with a lit horizon, a beautiful reunion was about to unfold.

About The Author

Jill Brooks Pellerin was born in Paducah, Kentucky in 1953, not even close to the ocean shore. Obtaining degrees in French Translation and Dental Hygiene did not follow the course of her deepest feelings….the love and compassion for God's living creatures. Living on Hilton Head Island, South Carolina for 30 years raised Jill's awareness of the endangered sea turtles who would lay their eggs on the Carolina shores.

Jill currently spends her time in Atlanta, Ga. And Venice, Fl. working as a dental hygienist. She has many passions for living fueled by her love of God and Christ.

She loves watercolor painting, running, triathlon, backpacking and hiking, tennis and all water sports. She has had two children: Louis and Lindsay. Lindsay created the beautiful illustrations in this book.

Jill is a member of the Coastal Wildlife Club as a volunteer on Turtle Patrol, Appalachian Trail Conservancy, Alta Tennis Club, and Triathlon Federation USA.